I0073950

Cultivating Customers

Small Business Lead Generation in a Digital Age

By Doug Staneart

Legal Notice

© Copyright 2010, Doug Staneart
All Rights Reserved.
No part of this book may be reproduced, stored in a
retrieval system, or transmitted by any means, electronic,
mechanical, photocopying, recording, or otherwise, without
written permission from the author.
ISBN: 978-0-9818257-9-3

Table of Contents

Why Every Entrepreneur Needs this Book... Yesterday!

Over a decade ago, I started my first business. Like most entrepreneurs, I had expertise in my industry and an idea, but not a whole lot of practical experience running a small business. The hardest part about getting started was trying to find my first client. Few customers wanted to be the first to experiment with an unproven small business.

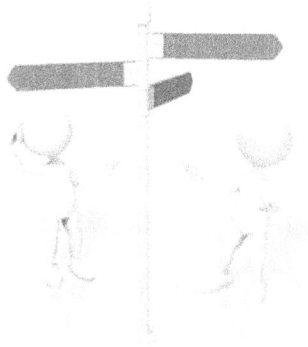

When successful professionals start their own businesses, it is kind of like a star athlete becoming a head coach. The coaching is something that the athlete is familiar with, but without the coaching experience, the athlete will probably struggle in the beginning. Some athletes make that transition better than others, and it's the same with entrepreneurs. There is a learning curve along the way – shorter for some business owners and longer for others, it's vitally important that this transition take place.

In my own situation, things eventually started rolling… slowly anyway, (even a blind hog can find a nut every once in a while, right?) but those first couple of years were really lean. I tried everything to try to get my business to grow, but I was starting to get very frustrated with the advice that I was getting from the "so called" experts.

Since I started my company, I've personally conducted hundreds of public speaking seminars, and I've, in fact, become pretty well recognized as one of the top presentation training instructors in the world. However, before anyone knew who I was or what The Leader's Institute® was, I had a hard time getting people to attend the class. So I decided to give a presentation seminar away for free. I figured that, even though I wasn't making any money, I could at least get great testimonials from the folks who I did the work for.

I printed up brochures, and I headed out to anywhere that I could find a group of people that would take one of my brochures. I went to the Chamber of Commerce business card exchanges, the Small Business Breakfast put on by the local university, the Rotary and Kiwanis clubs meetings, and I even infiltrated a few Toastmaster groups. In all, I had handed out over 1000 brochures promoting my free public speaking seminar. I was so excited, because I had really worked hard. I was expecting a really big turnout.

The day came. I got to the room very early to setup. I had told everyone to come a little early, because there was limited seating. When it got to be about fifteen minutes before the start time and no one was there yet, I began to get worried, though.

A couple of minutes before we were going to start, a woman that I had met from the All American Asian Chamber of Commerce showed up. (I know, I'm not Asian-American, but she told me that for a $50 membership fee, I could be one of the Chamber's founding members.) I remember letting out an audible, "Whew!" when she walked in. I greeted her warmly and asked her to have a seat.

She was a little shocked that no one else was there yet. (I was too, by the way.) I really hoped that we had a bunch of scared speakers sitting in their cars just waiting for the absolute last minute to come inside. So I made small talk with my first arrival.

I asked her what it was about public speaking that troubled her, just so I could better customize the seminar for her as we got started. She gave me a few vague responses. After a few questions, I just paused, and I asked her why she had really come.

She laughed and said that she really wasn't interested in the seminar. She had just come to network with the attendees (and try to get them to join her Chamber).

After another 15 minutes or so, I came to the horrifying conclusion that she was going to be my only attendee. Seriously... I tried to give away my expertise, and I only got one person to attend. (And she hadn't even come to hear me.)

Only having one person show up to my first class was an embarrassing failure, but I learned from the experience and moved on. I made lots of mistakes in the early years, and I worked really, really hard to grow my business.

I made lots of cold calls, joined Chambers of Commerce, I attended the business card exchanges, I attended (even led) the leads groups, I joined associations, I networked, I volunteered, I got elected to committees and boards, and I made a lot of good friends. I also wasted A LOT OF TIME and money, because most of the stuff that "they" told me to do was absolutely worthless in helping me grow my business.

After a while, I started looking at all of the people who were also doing these activities. They were all hard-working people, but they were also all broke. None of them had the kind of success that I was looking to achieve, and each of them had pretty much topped out at the standard of living that they were currently living at. So I made some changes.

This book was written to help all of those people who are struggling to get their small businesses started and who are getting absolutely frustrated with all of the business card exchanges that are fun to attend, but might be a waste of time otherwise. It was also written for those entrepreneurs who hate to cold call people. Finally, it's for those salt-of-the-Earth trend-setters who have fantastic ideas, but want to grow their business at a much, much faster rate.

The strategies and secrets in this book will keep you from making many of the most costly mistakes that almost every entrepreneur makes. Read on and greatly magnify your success as a business person!

Chapter 1:
The Top Ten Mistakes that Entrepreneurs Make (And How to Fix Them)

After the initial "start up struggles" when I first created my company, I began to start to get phone calls and emails out of the blue from people wanting to come and work for my trendy, up and coming company. One was from a pretty successful entrepreneur in Orlando, Rick Highsmith, who had already created and sold two companies. When he first called me and told me of some of his accomplishments, I paused and said, "And why is it again that you want to come work for me?" because he had already done what I was trying to do. I figured that I should probably be working for him.

After a few phone calls, Rick decided to invest in a flight to Los Angeles where my next class was taking place, and after the first few hours of the class, he was hooked. He and I had lunch at the hotel, and he told me how impressed that he was with the class. He said that he had "audited" about ten different training companies and had actually gotten certified to teach a few classes, but he wanted to be a part of The Leader's Institute® because what we were doing was so unique.

I smiled at him and said, "That's funny, because I decided to hire you the moment you bought your plane ticket to Los Angeles." No one had ever taken a risk like that on me, so I was very impressed.

Then I looked him right in the eye and said, "Great, that makes two of us now..." and his jaw dropped into his plate. He couldn't believe that I was running this huge, international company all by myself.

The truth was that, at that time, my company wasn't a huge international company. In fact, the previous year, the entire revenue of the company was only about $130,000 and the profit was a lot (lot, lot) less.

But I had already begun to figure a few things out about being a small business owner. The main thing was that when everyone else was paying fees to become a "Certified Small Business," I was beginning to create the impression in the marketplace that my company was a BIG business.

Like most entrepreneurs, I made a bunch of mistakes in the beginning, but every time that I made one of these mistakes, I learned something. Once I learned some of these secrets, I began to pass them along to other business owners so they didn't have to make the same mistakes.

Folks say that "Experience is the best teacher," but that is really only about half right. In fact, "Someone ELSE'S experience is the best teacher," because they have already made those mistakes. Learn from them, and you get to a higher level of success in a much faster time frame. Below are a list of mistakes that many entrepreneurs make, so learn from their mistakes and avoid these challenges.

The Top Ten Mistakes that Entrepreneurs Make (and How to Avoid Them)

Mistake #1: Hiding Your Company from the World

The internet is the great equalizer for small businesses, but you have to make it easy for people who are looking for your products or services to find you on the internet. Search engine optimization (making it easier for people to find your website through search engines like Google) should be your top priority as a small business owner.

Mistake #2: "I'm a Really Small Company" Website

Just like when a person hands you a business card with the rough edges from separating it at the perforation after it was printed at home, a cheap looking or homemade looking websites is a neon sign saying, "I'M A SMALL BUSINESS... Don't trust me."

Mistake #3: Creating a Confusing Perception in the Marketplace

This mistake made early in a business' history can follow you for years. When we first start out, we're trying to find any way that we can to generate revenue, so when times are tough in one product or service line, we dabble in others to make ends meet. People who see you promoting dissimilar product lines will wonder what exactly it is that you do.

Mistake #4: *I Can Do It on My Own* **Mentality**

We become entrepreneurs because we are experts in a specific industry, and we know that we can do it better than our competitors. However, we are never going to be experts in EVERYTHING, so it's important to surround yourself with other experts in different industries. You can either contract work out through subcontracting or joint ventures, or you can create alliances with other companies who support you but don't compete with you.

Mistake #5: Offering Something that the Market Doesn't Want

You might have a great product or service that people actually want to buy, but if you are promoting that product or service to a marketplace that doesn't want it, you'll go broke. If you are networking with other entrepreneurs and your services are for prime contractors, you'll just become very frustrated. Go find where people in your target market gather, and promote your company there instead.

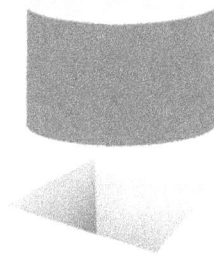

Mistake #6: Salesperson Fangs

This mistake is the absolute most annoying and will drive customers away in droves. It occurs when someone out of genuine interest or in some cases, just kindness asks a question about what the person does for a living, and in response, the person spends the next fifteen minutes talking about himself and how the listener really needs his product or service. Successful people tend to be pretty good listeners.

Mistake #7: Casting Your Pearls before Swine

Just so you know, I'm not calling your prospects swine. I'm just saying that most small business people spend way too much time with people who they think are prospects but who have absolutely no chance of ever buying something from them. In order to be a good prospect for you, the person needs to have the resources to buy from you and the authority to buy from you. Don't spend a lot of time and effort building a reputation amongst people who aren't in and will never be in your target market. Find where your market gathers and build your reputation there.

Mistake #8: Giving a Pitch Instead of Solving a Problem

Most people walk into a meeting with a prospect or start a call with a prospect with a pitch in mind. So, before the prospect even indentifies a problem or a need, the pitch starts and we verbally jump all over the person with features and benefits demonstrating how great our product is. Remember that a successful entrepreneur is one who solves problems for clients and customers, so spend less time talking about yourself and ask more questions about the prospect.

Mistake #9: No Follow Up (Web Visitors and Leads)

This used to be a big problem with face-to-face meetings where an entrepreneur collects a business card from a prospect and then just doesn't do anything with it. In the digital age, however, website visitor follow ups are way more valuable and rarely capitalized on effectively. Where in the past, we might collect 10 business cards at a meeting, now, we might get hundreds or thousands of people viewing our website every day. If we don't follow up on business cards, we might miss a sale or two, but if we don't capture contact information from website visitors, we're missing out on thousands of new customers.

For instance, if you look at most website statistics, you'll see a number of "page views" which is just the number of pages on your website that people have looked at in a given month. This number is almost always a BIG number, but then if you compare it with the number of people who actually request information from or buy from you, the latter is microscopic in comparison. More often than not, the big difference in numbers comes because we don't make it easy for people to request information from or contact us.

Mistake #10: Slow Follow-Up

In face-to-face meetings, if you don't follow up within 24 hours, your prospect will likely forget about most of your meeting because people are extremely busy. Website visitors are not as forgiving. If you don't respond to them within a few minutes, they will forget about you. When we surf the internet looking for solutions to our problems, we want instant gratification. If we don't get it, we just move on to the next site.

Follow up quickly with your prospects, and you'll increases sales dramatically.

If you solve just some of these challenges that many small businesses face, you'll increase your income potential and your growth rate very quickly. This book was created to offer tangible, step-by-step processes and ideas to conquer these and other obstacles that you'll likely face as you build your small business.

These tips were created through the "school of hard knocks" so if you follow this roadmap, you should be able to keep from having to make all of the mistakes that we had to in order to get to the top.

Success to you!

Chapter 2:
Why Spamming and Cold Calling Do Not Work

Every small business is the proverbial needle in the haystack, so small business lead generation is critical to an entrepreneur's survival and the growth of his/her small business. The thing that most entrepreneurs forget, though, is that it is a lot easier to turn a prospect or lead into a customer if the lead calls you versus when you call them.

It cracks me up when I hear titles of articles, seminars, or books about how to "Make Effective Cold Calls" or how to "Warm Up Cold Calls". These are great titles to peak interest, because everyone who has made calls like this in the past is desperate to find a better way to generate leads. However, cold calls, in general are a low return activity. Ask any salesperson if they would rather make 100 cold calls or receive a single call-in lead, and the salesperson will always choose the one call-in lead, because he/she has a better shot at closing the call-in lead.

If you haven't eaten for days and are really hungry, would you rather have 100 fishing poles on the same dock in the ocean or one pole fishing into a bucket of fish? If you have 100 poles, it is difficult to split your time to make you efficient, so in reality, you are just fishing with one pole in 100 different spots. You have a much better shot at eating if you fish into the bucket – especially if you get two or three (or 10, or 100) new buckets showing up on the dock every day.

What most business owners do is hire salespeople to make cold calls. They see the 100 poles and think that if they just get more people to operate the poles, then sooner or later, someone will get a bite. The flawed logic is that when one person does get lucky and catch a fish, you now have 10 fishermen to feed with it.

A better plan is to grow your team as your sales support them. If you have five or six buckets showing up every day, then you might now need help fishing in them. Increase your buckets, and your business will grow. If you increase your staff without being able to support them, you'll create a revolving door for your staff, and you will just increase your training and hiring costs.

In the past decade (through two recessions, mind you,) I've built a total of four multi-million dollar businesses from scratch, and none of that revenue was ever generated from any "cold call". In fact, I've had over 405 of the Fortune 500 companies become clients, and they have all called or emailed my companies, not the other way around. They searched my companies out when they had a problem. If I or my team of instructors had been cold calling within these same companies trying to find people that were facing the specific problems that we could solve, it would have been very costly and frustrating.

Below are a few of the secrets that we have uncovered to help small businesses generate more leads (and more quality leads) and get prospects to call you.

Cold Calls do not Work at All in a Digital Age

Cold calls, email spam, blast faxes, popup windows, forced "opt-in" subscribers and the like just don't work in this digital age (I'm not sure if any of them ever worked very well for very long). The companies that crack me up the most are those that send out blast email spam guaranteeing that they can get any website to the top of Google in 48 hours. Seriously? Do you think that if they could actually do this that they would be wasting their time spamming millions of people begging someone to buy their service?

> "The truth is that cold calling and spamming people shows desperation, not success."

Last month, over 165,000 people went to Google searching for the service that these spammers offer. If they could get to the top of Google like they claim, they would have about two million potential leads coming to them every year. So why would they need to spam people? "If you are so good at what you do, why are you spamming me? Why are you cold calling me? Why are you trying to force me to subscribe to your newsletter?" The truth is that cold calling and spamming people shows desperation, not success.

Get Potential Leads to Call You and Turn more Leads into Customers

The internet is the great equalizer for small businesses. Big businesses have websites, but their bureaucracy forces them to move very slowly in implementing new technology and capitalizing on new opportunities. However, nimble small businesses can capitalize on these opportunities immediately.

It is actually very easy to get to the top of a Google search result. It is very difficult, however, to stay there. In fact, it is a fulltime job. But it is a very lucrative fulltime job. Logically, this is why this is your most important goal for your small business.

> *When someone has a question, where do they go for an answer now?*

In decades past, if you had a challenge or a question, you might ask a friend or coworker, or if it was a really big problem, you might go to the library and do some research. Today, though, people go immediately to Google. The listings at the top of the first page have a lot more credibility than the ones on the second, third, or four-hundredth.

If your small business is listed at the top of the results when searchers enter their keywords or phrase, and they click through to your website and get the answer to their question, then your small business is now at the top of their short-list for solution providers. If they call or email you, then you automatically have about a pretty good chance of turning that lead into a client. In contrast, if your small business is listed at the top of page two on Google, in order to have someone contact you, they will have already looked at listings from at least 10 other competitors. Most potential customers will not be that thorough, so you will generate fewer leads, and now, since you are competing with at least ten other competitors, your percentage of closing drops to below 10%.

Let me reiterate that, because it is a critical point. It's like when I was a kid and my dad was teaching me how to pick a good watermelon at the supermarket. He lightly thumped the outside of about five or six watermelons listening for that hallow echo that told him that the watermelon was ripe. While Dad was being choosey looking for the perfect melon, other people came up and picked one off of the top and walked away. Oddly enough, no one dug through 40 or 50 watermelons down to the bottom looking for the perfect melon. Your prospects won't either. They will either take the one off the top or, if they are a little more thorough, choose from the few at the top.

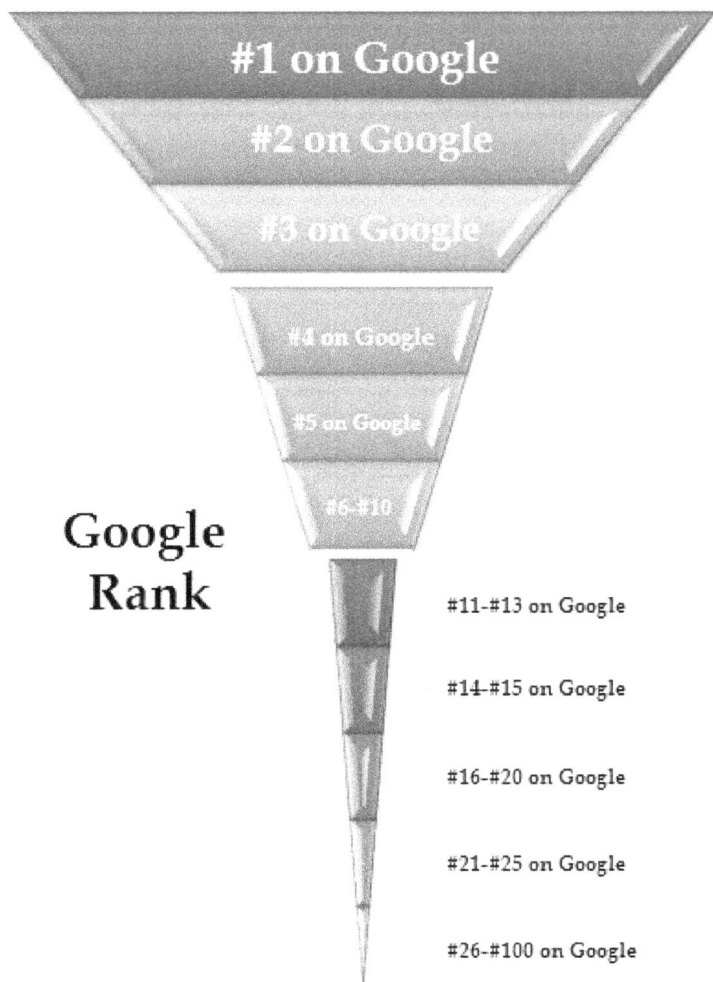

#1 on Google

#2 on Google

#3 on Google

#4 on Google

#5 on Google

#6-#10

Google Rank

#11-#13 on Google

#14-#15 on Google

#16-#20 on Google

#21-#25 on Google

#26-#100 on Google

Number of Leads in Your Sales Funnel

The Bigger Your Funnel (Higher Your Ranking),
the More Leads You will Generate

Some (a few) will only look at the first listing on Google, click through, and find exactly what they want. A much larger number will click through to the top three or the top five listings. A small percentage will click through to every listing on the first page to make sure they are being thorough. A microscopic portion of the population will click to the second page and do additional research.

The thing to keep in mind is that if you are in the top spot on Google, EVERY ONE of those people will see your website. If you are in the top three listings, most will see your website (maybe 75% or so). If you are number six through ten on the first page, maybe 25% of the searchers will see you, and out of that 25%, your website will be compared with the other nine listings in the top ten, so your closing ratio will be much smaller. If you are on page two, well... you get the picture. (It's much harder to generate leads.)

Later on in the book, we'll give you a number of simple strategies that will help boost your website's popularity and increase your rankings.

Get Leads to Call You by Giving Away Something that They Need or Want

What is common knowledge to you is uncommon to most people. Remember that your expertise, your knowledge, is extremely valuable to people who are searching on Google for answers as in the previous example. So if you can help them answer the question – and really help them in the process – they are more likely to share their contact information with you. Once they do, you now know two things about them. First, you know that they have (or had) a specific problem that you can help them solve. Second, they know who you are and trust that you are an expert in your industry.

> "What you give away doesn't have to be costly, but it must have value for your customer."

What you give away doesn't have to be costly, but it must have value for the customer. When I say "Costly," I mean that what you give away, ideally, won't cost anything for you to produce it. For instance, if you have a lot of informational content on your blog, then you might ask people to register in order to conduct a search of your blog for specific topics. Or, you might give away a special report or access to a video or audio file with information that a prospect might need.

If you are a dentist, you might offer a video about how to teach a three-year-old to brush properly. Anyone who requests the free information will likely have a young child and be concerned about the child's oral health. The only cost that the dentist will incur is the initial recording cost, if the dentist uploads the file to a website. No matter how many people download the file, the dentist doesn't incur any more cost.

You could make a video like this with your cell phone and upload it to YouTube for free, or you could hire a professional videographer to come to your office and really do a great job on the recording for a couple hundred bucks. Either way, once the video is made, it doesn't cost you anything when someone views it. If a million people watch the video on your website, then you will no additional costs.

Whatever the gift, just make sure that your costs are low and the value of the item is high from the customer's perspective.

This is an important point. My uncle is a successful entrepreneur in his own right, and he and I were discussing ideas about generating new clients at a family dinner a few months ago. He owns a very prestigious golf club in Ireland, and he had just published his first book and was very excited about it.

I mentioned to him that if he were to create a PDF version of his book, he could sell it on Amazon for the Kindle or on the iPad Marketplace, and he wouldn't have any of the costs associated with printing the book, and he was intrigued. However, when I mentioned that he could give a copy of this PDF book away as an incentive to come out as a paying guest and play a round of golf at his club, he balked.

He said, "No I have a friend at another club who hired a consultant to increase his membership, and the consultant made him give free rounds of golf away to increase membership. The consultant told him that once people come out and play a round, they would definitely want to become members."

I could see what was coming, and I said, "Well, that doesn't sound like a great plan... What happened?"

He told me that because his friend's club was a very prestigious club, he got hundreds and hundreds of people responding to the free offer, and the club was crowded for months even though they ended the promotion after only a few days. The current members began to get frustrated, because their tee times were being affected by the freebies.

When I asked him how many new members that the promotion generated, he responded with, "Well, I'm not sure, but not nearly enough to justify the challenges."

The owner of the club made a couple of big mistakes. First, the free offer definitely had a lot of value, but it was also VERY costly. Every time a free foursome came to play at his club, it impacted the regular members.

In addition, the people who he gave the free rounds of golf to were not necessarily the market that would invest in a golf membership at a prestigious club. For instance, let's say you are a person who would never join a club because you are pretty satisfied playing at your municipal courses, and you don't really have the money to invest in a high-dollar membership. However, you hear that one of the best clubs in the country is giving away free rounds of golf. It's a once-in-a-lifetime opportunity for you, and it's FREE! Of course you'd take them up on the offer, but you'd never be able to join the club.

A better choice of free gift for this club owner might be to have the golf pro record a series of golf tips videos and give them away when people register with his website. (Or my uncle could give a PDF version of his book away for people who register with his own site.) Now he would have a list of people who are interested in his course, and he can send out promotions to them. A free bucket-of-balls for the driving range when they play a round of golf might be a way to get this specific group of people to the club and weed out the non-buyers who are just looking for more free stuff.

So forget the cold calls and spam, use your website to get more leads to call you, and then use a high-valued free gift to encourage prospects to contact you, and you will generate great success through small business lead generation.

Chapter 3:
The Truth about Networking and Business Card Exchanges

Word-of-mouth advertising is one of the cheapest and most effective types of advertising your company can invest in, but how do we generate this elusive type of advertising?

Most experts in the area will say, "Get out and 'network'." So we go to a Chamber of Commerce meeting with dozens or even hundreds of other people trying to promote their company or service, and we attempt to promote our company or service as well. Very few people come to these meetings to buy things. The odds seem to be stacked against from the beginning, so is it any wonder why most of us come back from these meetings thinking that we just wasted an hour or two?

It's like walking into a shooting range and looking down at your shirt and seeing dozens of red laser dots. The odds are against you.

It doesn't have to be that way. By making just a few simple changes to our approach, we can become a center of influence in any room and, in effect, generate significant word of mouth advertising. One of the first things that we have to realize, though, is what 'networking' actually is and what it is not.

Networking IS NOT selling.

If we know 99% of the people at a networking function are there to promote their own product or service (not buy from us,) and we try to sell our product or service to them, we are likely to frustrate (and bore) ourselves and the people we are talking with.

Networking IS increasing our sphere of influence in order to promote our product or service to this sphere of influence at a future time. People aren't going to buy anything from or refer their friends to someone that they don't trust. So our goal during a networking function is not to sell, but to get more people to like and trust us. That way, they are more likely to buy from us in the future or refer people to us. One way to get people to trust us more is to help them get what they want.

One of my good friends, Bob Burg, wrote a book called *Endless Referrals*, and he gave some of the best networking advice ever.

People like other people who are interested in them. The most important topic to anyone you are speaking to is himself or herself. And since they are at the meeting to promote their product or service, if we help them do that better, then they are going to like us and trust us more. The following questions are things that Burg suggests that you ask someone at a networking function that will get them to open up to you and tell you about themselves:

- What is your name? Obviously a first question.
- What do you do? Still nothing out of the ordinary.
- Do you travel much? What territory do you work in? Any question about location.

- What do you like most about what you do? Keeps the conversation positive and gives you more insight about the person and his/her company.
- What makes you or your company unique or different from your competition? Let them brag.
- What are some of your accomplishments or things you are proud of? Let them brag more.
- How would I know if someone I was talking to would be a good prospect for you? This one question can make you more money than any other you can ask.

These questions will help you really get to know the person and what he or she can do. With this type of information at your fingertips (and it is a good idea to write the information down--possible on the back of a business card,) as you network, eventually you will come across someone who would be a good prospect for that person. The moment you introduce those two people, you become a center of influence in that room. Do this just a couple of times, and the word will spread very quickly about how YOU are the person that everyone needs to know.

What makes this process so successful is the third party endorsement. The person who you are helping to promote his or her product or service is no longer struggling to find a warm prospect, now they are receiving a third party endorsement from you. That gives that person tremendous credibility to the prospect. You are helping both parties. These people tend to remember this type of help, and they return the favor ten-fold.

Eventually, you'll walk into a room, and people you have never even met before will begin bringing prospects to you. The key to making this process work is consistency and the ability to catalogue information about the people you meet. If you create a system that works for you, you will dramatically increase the word-of-mouth advertising about your company.

The key to networking is to be genuinely interested in the other person and do everything that you can to help the other person succeed at finding new prospects or solve problems. Do these things continuously, and you'll quickly become a center of influence.

Social Media Networking

If you attend every business card exchange or lead group in your city for a whole year, you might collect a couple of hundred leads. Since most of the leads that you accumulate came to the same function to sell to you, there is a good chance that it will be hard to create customers out of most of them. However, by networking on social media sites like Facebook or Linked-In, you can generate hundreds (or thousands) of high quality leads in one afternoon.

Doesn't that sound like more fun?

> "...every 10,000 people on your email list is worth $1,000,000 per year in potential income."

In order to build your social media network, the first step is to build your online presence so that new people are constantly finding your website and social media pages. A friend of mine in the internet marketing business told me that every 10,000 people on your email list is worth one million dollars per year in potential income. The bigger you list becomes, the more potential income you can generate from your list.

A sphere of influence who has a big list of people who opted in to his/her email list can pretty much write his/her own check every month and generate an unlimited amount of income.

For instance, let's say that you are a printing company, and you collect 1000 people who have either requested information about or bought business cards from you. Well, people who need business cards might also need advertising specialties like pens or magnets (or magnetic business cards). So you partner with a small business owner who sells advertising specialties that you met at a business card exchange, and you send an email out to your list offering a special deal for these advertising specialties. Even if only a few people respond, your new friend now has a number of new leads and new pieces of business because of the relationship that he has with you. You now have a new good friend.

Do you think that people who buy pens for their company might also have a need for business cards? You might be able to convince your new friend to offer your services to his list as well.

So how do you build your Facebook followers or Linked-In connections? Pretty much the same way. Every once in a while send out a notice to your followers asking them to "Like" a friend's website or Facebook page. Then ask them to do the same for you.

Other Facebook Tips

- Create a Fan Page. Any business can create a fan page (a "page") on Facebook, and it works just like a second website. However, anyone who "Likes" your page will get automatic updates when you post anything new to your site. So, you no longer have to collect email addresses and send out potential spam to your list. Just post something to your Facebook page, and everyone who has "Liked" you gets a copy of it instantly.

- If you ask people to help you, they are more likely to do so than if you just wait for them to help you. So, when you post something to your Facebook page, add a "If you like this click the LIKE button" notation.

- Post a list of ten articles and/or videos to your wall and send out an email to your contact list promoting the great content. Then ask them to help other viewers by LIKING the one of the ten items that they think was most helpful. CAUTION: Every time you post something to your Facebook page, anyone who has "Liked" you gets a copy on his/her Facebook page, so when you create your initial ten posts, either do it before you have any followers or post them one at a time every couple of days or so. Otherwise, you'll end up accidentally spamming your new followers.

- Add a "Like Button" application to your website or blog, so that people who read your site can promote you to their list. If you have a Wordpress website, go to Plugins and search for Facebook. You'll find plenty of options. If you have another type of website, go to www.facebook.com and scroll down to the bottom and click the Developers link and follow the instructions.
- Suggest friends to clients and colleagues. As you help them connect, you'll build trust.
- If you know a little about HTML and websites, make sure and use the FBML application to create custom web pages on your Facebook page. You are only limited by your creativity, but make the custom pages something that your fans will like and refer other people to. By the way, if you don't know a lot about HTML, then you can hire someone off of websites like www.elance.com to write code for you for very little money.
- We are just scratching the surface of the power of Facebook. This website is set to become the most powerful tool of the future for business.
- By the way, make sure and "Like" our page at www.facebook.com/tlibootcamp

Linked-In Tips

Linked-In is an extremely valuable networking tool for the business professional. Basically, it is a page that lets you post your business credentials, blog items, experience, etc. and lets you connect with other professionals that you know.

Once you connect with someone, you gain access to all of their connections in a graphic form. So if you sold a product to a department head at a big Fortune 500 company and connect with this person on linked-In, you'll be able to see who all of the other department heads are in that person's network.

Below are a few tips.

- Ask everyone that you meet if they have a Linked-In profile. If they say, "Yes", send them an invitation. If they say, "No" tell them about Linked-In and send them an invitation anyway.
- Ask for recommendations. When you work with people that you connect with, ask them to recommend you. If you think about the example I gave above with the department heads at the big company, that one recommendation can open many doors for you. All of your recommendations get listed on your Linked-In homepage, so when people view your page to "check you out," if you have

one recommendation, you have a little credibility. However, if you have 30 or 40 recommendations, you have a lot of credibility.

- Join strategic groups and add to the discussions. Search the groups for a keyword related to your industry. I typed in "Public Speaking" and got dozens of groups. Once you get to know people in the group and compliment them in your posts, then ask them to connect with you as well.

- Connect with me on Linked-In at www.linkedin.com/in/dougstaneart. For the connection, just list other and "Read book", and I'll approve the connection.

Twitter Tips

I have to admit that I'm not a big fan of Twitter, but it is a great way to connect with a big network of people, and with a little effort, you can build a large group. The best way to describe Twitter is that it's a texting platform like on cell phones, but it's on the web. Postings are limited to just a sentence or two at a time so short and sweet is most effective.

One of the great things about Twitter is that unlike the other two social websites, you don't have to know the people that you are connecting to. Just go onto their feed and FOLLOW them. After you do, anything that they post will get fed to your page. If they follow you, they will see your postings.

One of the interesting things about Twitter is that when you follow someone, they will often follow you back. So you can create a following pretty quickly – even if you are brand new to the site.

Search for postings with keywords related to your expertise, and when you find them, follow them.

And of course, publish your Twitter page URL to your website and business cards.

Social Networking is the Future

Social websites like these three examples are a great way to save a lot of time and connect with hundreds or thousands of prospects instantly. As you build your networks, you can easily promote special offers to them, share information, survey them, and much, much, more. Build your network and build your income!

Chapter 4:
Paying for Leads can Either Make You Rich or Close Your Business

Small business lead generation using pay-per-click ads can be very challenging. In fact, paying for leads can either make you really rich or drive you out of business.

Google makes a ton of money every year from pay-per-click ads. Most of the money that they make from these ads did not generate a single bit

of additional revenue for the companies or entrepreneurs who purchased them. However, there are a few people out in the business world who pay a little bit of money to Google and generate millions of dollars in return. They don't generate this type of income by accident. These entrepreneurs just have a better strategy than the ones who end up losing money on pay-per-click ads.

How to Lose Money in Pay-Per-Click Ads

The Uninformed Entrepreneur says, "I am not making money from my website because I'm not getting enough visitors, so I will invest in pay-per-click ads and that will make me money."

No, that will cost you hundreds or thousands of dollars every week with very little, if any, return on your investment. Effective advertising leverages or magnifies the return that you are already getting from your current sales channels. If your website is not generating leads or business for you before you invest in advertising, then you will be magnifying a zero return. 300% of zero is still zero.

When I was a kid, my dad saw me working hard on a hot day mowing the lawn, and he smiled and said, "You've done so well that I'm going to double your allowance this week."

"Cool! That's aweso... hey, wait a minute... I don't get an allowance," I replied back.

"In that case, I'll triple it," he said.

If you're not making money off your website and you invest in advertising, you're just paying good money after bad. If you double your sales, you probably won't even notice it.

Most people use pay-per-click ads as the starting point, and when they do, they will almost always lose money. They are betting their business capital on an untested experiment. It would be like buying a thoroughbred and running down to the racetrack and betting a bunch of money on your horse's first race. Yes, you would know what your horse is capable of, but your horse is untested against other horses. However, if your horse wins his first three races, you might want to invest a little on his fourth one.

Your website is the same way. Develop your website to where you are generating leads and sales from those leads. Then, once you have a track record of success, invest in pay-per-click ads. Now you are betting on a sure thing.

How to Generate Lots of Revenue from Pay-Per-Click Advertising

The Informed Entrepreneur says...

> *"I have finally got my business generating new leads from the internet, and now I want to leverage the success that I am currently having."*

Now you can make an informed budget for your pay-per-click advertising.

Here is a highly simplified example. If you are generating 10 leads per week from your website, and you are averaging closing one of those leads for $100 in revenue and $25 in profit, then you could only afford to pay $2.50 per lead to break even. Remember that just because someone clicks your pay-per-click link, does not mean that they will contact you and become a lead. If you have a fantastic website, you might be able to turn one out of every ten clicks into leads, so you could pay no more than $.25 per click to just break even. So pay-per-click won't work for you yet. You would need to increase the revenue per customer, or the profit margin, or the closing ratio (or all three) to make pay-per-click more cost effective for you.

If you invest in an email follow up system and generate the same 10 leads per week, this time you might turn three of those leads into customers. Since you are now able to build a longer term relationship with your leads, you might be able to bundle a few of your products together and generate a higher revenue per sale and increase your average sale to $300. By doing all of this, your cost per lead goes down dramatically. Now for every sale you are generating $100 in profit. With three sales out of ten leads, you generate a total of $300 in profit. You can now afford to pay $30 per lead, so with the same ten clicks turning into one lead, you could afford to pay up to $3 for each click. If you can get quality clicks for just $1 each, you will triple your pay-per-click investment.

So forget the cold calls and spam, use your website to get more leads to call you, and then use pay-per-click to leverage your success, and you will generate great success through small business lead generation.

I know what you're thinking... So how do I get people to visit my website in the first place? Well, Chapter Five will show you a number of strategies that will help you. Since most people rely almost entirely on pay-per-click ads to funnel people to their website and that can be costly let's focus on how to lower that cost right away.

Writing Pay-Per-Click Ads that Lead to Sales

Once you have a great site and follow up system set up, now you can insert some ads. Remember that the goal is NOT to get people to click your ad. The goal is to get people who will buy something from you to click your ad.

For instance, if I make an ad that says...

> *"One out of every 100 people who click this link will win $1000,"*

I'd get a LOT of clicks. However, none of them would buy anything from me, so I'd just lose a lot of money. Or, if I am a local dentist in Frisco, Texas, and I place an ad that says, "Free Teeth Whitening Tips," I'll also get a lot of clicks, but very few sales. Most of the people who click will just want the free tips, and very few of them will be in my local neighborhood. A better ad would say something like, "Frisco, TX Dentist – Free teeth cleaning with your first whitening treatment." If you don't want to go to a dentist in Frisco, TX, you are less likely to click that link. People who do click the link are probably pretty good prospects for you.

You will always have numb-skulls who click your links even though they don't need or want anything that you are promoting, but you'll have fewer people click your paid-for links who are looking for something different than what you are offering.

Before you attach your credit card to an ad, though, test it. Then test some more. Then, once you have tested, test everything again.

For instance, you might want to create 10 different ads and run each of them a couple of days at a time to see which works best for you. Then use the tools that Google provides to see how many clicks were generated, how many leads developed from the clicks, how much each click coast you, and how much revenue you generated from the investment. Whichever one gives you the best return on your investment is the one that you might start with.

So if you want to generate more leads for your small business using pay-per-click, make your website and follow up system solid first, then use effective ads to target the specific market who will buy your services.

Chapter 5:
Optimize Your Website
Offer What People Want

How do you know what your customers really, really want? In years past, you might have conducted an intense survey by sending out thousands of survey mailers to potential customers hoping that enough people send them back to you to create a valid survey sample. Because that was such a time-consuming and expensive process, almost no one ever did it, so we got creative.

I remember Wendy's used to leave comment cards on every table along with a small wooden box on the wall to deposit it into. American Airlines sends out gratitude cards to their frequent fliers to give to their employees when they go above and beyond the call of duty in service.

But for the most part, we used to just guess. If we guessed right, we made a lot of money. If we guessed wrong, we lost a lot of money.

Today though, you can instantly find out what a massive group (millions of people) really want in a matter of seconds and at absolutely no cost... And everyone has access to it.

What is the one word solution to finding out what people really want?

G-O-O-G-L-E.

Yup, just like most things in life today, there is an answer in Google. The best tool I've ever found is the Google Keyword Suggestion Tool located at:

https://adwords.google.com/select/KeywordToolExternal (Or just type *Google Keyword Tool* into Google).

This keyword tool is really magical, and it will be your best friend when you create or refurbish your website, your social media pages, your articles or videos, and your advertising messages. Here's what you do.

First, go to the Keyword Tool and type in a few keywords or phrases related to what you do. For instance, if you are a mechanical contractor, you might type in...

Air conditioning
HVAC
Heating and Air
Mechanical contracting

...and conduct your search. When you get the results, click the "Local Monthly Searches" link at the top of one of the columns. This will sort your results from most popular to least popular.

What you are looking for in the results are keywords or phrases that people enter into Goggle looking for your company. If you are a mechanical contractor, the most popular phrases are heater, air conditioner, air conditioning, etc. You'll want to make sure that anytime you write ANYTHING on your website, Facebook page, articles, etc., that you use a few of these key phrases.

The more important thing that you are looking for is what are called "long tail keywords." These are a string of keywords or phrases that are MUCH easier to optimize your website to target. For example, if your main keyword is "air conditioning" you will be competing with millions of webpages all over the world for search engine popularity. Even if you are really good, it will be very difficult to get to page one for that search term.

Instead, choose a couple of "long tail keywords" like the following:

Air conditioner in Texas
Air conditioner Dallas, TX
Air conditioner repair Dallas, TX
Air conditioner service repair Dallas, TX

Every time you add a new word to your long tail, you increase the chance that you can corner the market on the phrase, however you decrease the chance that anyone will ever enter it into Google. So it is a balancing act. Maybe only one person every two months will enter "air conditioner service repair Dallas TX" into Google, but every time that they do, your website shows up as number one on the list.

If I were going to choose phrases to make long tails out of based on what showed up in my Google Keyword Tool search, I'd include these terms:

Duct cleaning

Fix air conditioner
Thermostat
Air conditioner problems

The reason why these phrases are good choices is that each of these keywords were entered into Google over 75,000 last month, and I bet that very few of the other mechanical contractors are targeting those keywords on their website (at least not prominently).

All of those competitors are using "air conditioner repair," but none are using "fix air conditioner" because it can't be used very well in proper grammar. So if this were my company, I'd title one of the pages of my website something like...

Fix Air Conditioner Problems within 24 Hours

...by doing this, I'm using two of those four phrases at the same time.

Do a Keyword Tool search right now for words related to your industry and make two lists. Make the first list the four or five top keywords or phrases that people entered. On the second list, write down four or five long tail potential keywords or phrases.

After you make your list, go back to your website and search for the number of times that those words show up anywhere on your site. This will give you a good idea of how much work you have to do to make your website easier for people to find you.

Your list will also help you start to help the people who are looking for you as well. If you want to add articles or videos to your blog, you now have your topics and titles.

So possible articles or video titles for the above example would be something like:

- Duct Cleaning 101: Step-by-Step Air Duct Cleaning
- The Top Five Air Conditioning Problems
- Check the Thermostat of your Air Conditioning Company
- Quick Fix Air Conditioner Solutions to Common Problems

Post these articles or videos on your blog or Facebook page, and two things will happen. First, you'll get the natural hits from Google. Second, if the articles have good information, then they will get passed around and you might get calls or emails just from the articles themselves.

The Google Keyword Tool is the key to making sure that what you are offering is what the market is actually looking for. Use it wisely and often!

Chapter 6:
Get Your One-Page Ad on 1000 Website in 30 Days (For Free!)

A couple of months ago, I started looking at hiring a fulfillment company to duplicate and send out all of our home study courses, MP3 disks, and books, etc. Since I wasn't sure where to start, I sent an email out to one of my friends who is also a professional speaker asking who he used, but I got impatient waiting for a response. So I did a quick Google search as well.

The top eight or nine listings were all fulfillment companies and all seemed pretty much the same on their websites. Toward the bottom of the page, there was a listing titled, "How to Pick a Dependable Fulfillment Company," and when I clicked it, I found an article with a few things to look for when making my decision. At the bottom of the article was information about the author, and she worked for one of the companies that was in the top three listings on the page.

I clicked through to the listing, and figured that this particular company was probably a good company to call first. A few minutes after I made the phone call, I got a response back from my friend recommending the same company.

I've got to tell you, I felt pretty confident hiring this company. It was a "no-brainer" now.

I hired the company because when I was confused and needed help, the information that this company provided gave me a solution. In addition, my friend's recommendation just sealed the deal.

Your Expertise is Valuable – And Needed

The internet has opened up a tremendous opportunity for you to become the "go to" expert in your industry.

Every industry has associations, trade publications, how-to websites, forums, blogs, newsletters, and more. And each of those entities has at least one major thing in common... They constantly need articles, studies, and white papers for their online and off-line publications. A lot of these publications are published weekly or monthly (and in some cases – daily) so they are ALWAYS looking for fresh material.

This is where you come in. Remember, what is common knowledge for you is un-common to everyone else. So if you give these entities what they need, they will make you famous (at least in your industry.)

Article Directories are Your Billboard

So if you are a blogger, the editor of a weekly or monthly newsletter, or even the person at a company who puts together bulletins for your team, you constantly have the same problem. "What the heck am I going to print this week?"

The internet has solved this problem for you too, though. There dozens and dozens of article directories on the internet whose sole purpose is to store and catalogue articles and blog entries so that when someone like the newsletter editor above needs an article in a pinch, all this person would need to do is conduct a search on just about any topic.

Once the article gets catalogued, it's going to be on that website forever. Granted, the newer articles are always more popular in search engines, but the older articles stick around too.

So how do you get your article on 1000 websites?

It's pretty easy, actually. Pick 25 article directories that are most likely to accept your article. The easy way to do this is to type "Submit Your Article" into Google and add a keyword to it to narrow down the searches to directories that would accept your topic. So enter "Submit your article air conditioning."

If you submit your article to these 25 directories, within a few days, it will show up on their homepage (at least for a short time, then it will move to an internal page of the website). Each of these directories have hundreds or thousands of publishers searching for content. If just one of those editors republish your article, you'll be on

50 web pages very quickly (25 directories and 25 newsletters or blogs).

Next, post the article to your blog and Facebook page. If you just have 100 followers, the article will show up on all 100 of their Facebook pages. Here is where leverage works phenomenally. If just ONE of those 100 people click the "Like" button on Facebook, the article summary now gets reposted on all of their friends' pages as well, so if they have 100 friends, you get 100 more impressions.

That is a VERY conservative 250 total web pages on which your article is now being published. So just do that same thing once per week for four weeks, and you'll have a one-page ad on 1000 different websites in less than 30 days – and it's all FREE!

By the way, there are services on the web that will automatically submit your articles to directories for you. Submit Your Article is actually a UK company that does a pretty good job. You can find them online at http://www.tli-submityourarticle.com

Another service that gets great reviews is Submit Edge at http://www.submitedge.com/1396.html. They are a fee for service website so if you want one article submitted, they charge you one fee versus a subscription service. You pay for the number of sites that they submit to up to 400 websites. So if you are just starting, you might test your articles here and then change to a subscription service when you are consistently writing articles every week.

The Snowball Effect

Those numbers that I gave you above are really conservative. If a couple of more newsletters republish your article, if you have more than 100 followers on Facebook, or if you ask your followers to click the "Like" button and a larger number do click it, then you'll be published on a much greater number of websites.

Here's how it worked for me. When I first started my company, I was broke. I didn't have money to spend on advertising. Well, actually I did buy an ad in the newspaper that was running a couple of times a week for a month or so, and I lost tens of thousands of dollars in a very short time – money that I really didn't have by the way. So I wrote about 12 articles instead.

I didn't write them all at once. It took me about six months. This was in the days before Facebook, so the only outlet that I had was individual newsletters and article directories (which were in their infancy back then). Within a year, those 12 articles were republished onto over 14,000 websites, and my company moved to the top of Google in three different categories (Public speaking courses, leadership training, and team building.)

"Once my company got to that top spot, we no longer had to go out and search for new clients."

Once my company got to that top spot, we no longer had to go out and search for new clients. Hundreds of people were calling us and emailing us every week. I no longer had to search for new employees. I was receiving dozens of resumes and a few phone calls every week from people wanting to join my company, so I got to choose from the cream-of-the-crop. The longer that we were in the top spot, the faster we grew.

This last section was literally the secret to the success of my company. If you do nothing else that I recommend to you, go back and re-read this chapter over and over and do what I'm suggesting to you. You will make a fortune if you do.

What Do You Write About?

- Problems that you/your team have solved that would be helpful to others.

- How-To instructions for something that you do.

- Myths or misunderstood aspects of your industry.

- Trends in your industry.

- Advice to Customers.

- Anything else of interest to people in your industry.

(And of course the topics that you discovered when you did your Keyword Tool search!)

How Do You Write a Good Article?

1. Choose a Topic of Interest to Your READER (not self-fulfilling for you.) Choose a topic from the previous page as a guideline.
2. Identify the three to five most important key points that the reader would need to know about your topic.
3. For each of the major points, add a story, some data, a quote from an expert, or some other piece of evidence to make a complete paragraph.
4. Add an introduction to the beginning of the article outlining the three to five major points.
5. Add a conclusion to the end of the article summarizing the key points one more time.
6. Promote yourself in the "author box" at the conclusion.

That's it. Easy. An article should have 600 to 1000 words, but if you have three to five points and some good evidence, the article will pretty much write itself.

What Happens if You Can't Write?

Keep in mind that most of the editors of these newsletters are really desperate, so your writing doesn't really have to be great. In fact, it doesn't even necessarily have to be any good. If it has the correct keywords and a link pointing back to your website, it will work.

But if you really want to make the best impression, you have a couple of choices. An easy way to write articles is to just carry a recorder around with you and go to a friend or coworker and explain something to that person related to your topic. Then, just transcribe the audio file. Clean it up, and you'll have a descent article.

Another option is to network with other entrepreneurs and coach each other. In our boot camps, we organize weekly teleseminars where attendees can call in and the group helps the members organize their articles better.

You can also pay people to write the articles for you. A lot of our coaching members just send our instructors their ideas, and we write and publish their articles for them. You can also go to websites like eLance.com and find contractors to write articles for you.

So it's pretty easy. Just get started.

Chapter 7:
Become a Movie Star and Funnel Leads to Yourself

One of my friends, Mike Koenigs, opened up a whole new world to me a couple of years ago, and his ideas have been a very exciting edition to my company. According to recent Nielsen reports, the average age of television viewers is over the age of 50. The younger that a person is, the more likely he/she will go to YouTube versus network TV when he/she has free time.

Web videos are becoming a vital part of an online presence. They are also a stimulating way to engage new prospects for your business.

I met Mike Koenigs at a seminar a couple of years ago, and he has a simple step-by-step process to best use internet video sites to drive traffic to your website. In fact, Mike calls his company, Traffic Geyser. He has a number of free videos about how to do videos at http://www.tli-trafficgeyser.com, but here is a brief summary of what he teaches.

Make Videos of Your FAQ's

Make a list of the questions that customers most frequently ask you, and then make a second list of questions that, if they knew more about what you really do, your customers should be asking you.

Once you have your lists, take a video camera, digital snapshot camera set on the video setting, or even just your cell phone and record yourself asking the question and then answering it.

Make it easy, just start with, "One of the most frequently asked questions that we get when we are out in the field is…" and then just answer the question. Use a video editor like Windows Movie

Maker and add a title frame and an ending frame that just has the question and your website on it.

A couple of years ago, my wife and I bought a new house that has a nice pool in the backyard. Now, I've never had a pool, so the previous owner offered to come by and show me how to maintain it. He came out and said, "Do this and this and this and this, and of course if this happens, flip this switch, never do this, etc." So when he finished, my head was spinning, and he asked me if I had any questions. Of course, I said, "No," because I'm a man, and I have pride.

A couple of month later when the pool was green, I called the pool guys out. They told me that they had a "pool school" where they would teach me everything that I needed to know about the pool. I had a flashback to my crash course with the previous owner, and the pool technician could tell that I was a little apprehensive. He said, "If you want, you can just record me giving you the pool school," and I perked up.

I've referred back to that little video probably six or seven times when different things popped up. Just think of how many additional hits on their website this company would have created if they just videotaped this pool school themselves and put it on their web. You can do something similar with your business.

Once you have created the videos, just add them to your blog or website. If you want to leverage the content, upload it to all of the video websites that you can. There are now hundreds of them including YouTube.com. If you register with Traffic Geyser, Mike has software that will actually upload the video to dozens of websites for you. He charges you a monthly fee, but if you use the service, the return that you get will far outweigh the investment. (By the way, he just added an article submission service as well, so if you work with his website, you won't need to subscribe to an article submission service.)

I'm pretty loyal to Mike, because he's the guy who gave me the idea, and everything that he has shared with me has been spot on, but there are other services out there as well that can help. Here is a list of video submission services.

- Traffic Geyser – http://www.tli-trafficgeyser.com Traffic Geyser is a comprehensive service, but the best thing that they offer the small business person is education about how to make and submit videos. Mike used his own advice and created dozens of FAQ videos that give a step-by-step process for someone getting started. If you've never done video submission before, start here for a year or so, then if you want to switch to manual submissions, you'll make fewer mistakes.

- Video Submission – http://www.videosubmission.com I've never used this site, but their claim to fame is that they manually submit all of your videos, and they are a fee for service website versus a subscription service. So if you want to submit one video to 25 websites, you pay them $15, and someone on their staff manually submits them.
- Manual – http://www.manualvideosubmission.com/ Just like the last one, but a higher fee. If you want to do manual submissions you might try each and see which one does a better job.

Get Creative and Stand Out

Once you create your FAQ videos, now what? Your videos are only limited by your creativity. I'm always on the lookout for unique things that other people will find of interest.

For example, I taught a class in Frankfurt, Germany a few months ago, and while I was there, a volcano in Iceland erupted closing the airspace above Europe. I was trapped in Europe for an additional six days, and I had no plans because it was impromptu. So I took my camera and started riding the train to different cities making recordings and then tying the recordings to some kind of teaching in my industry.

View an example of one of these videos is at: http://www.youtube.com/watch?v=Ur_Woy4DgnE

I also take videos on vacations. In the first five years of my business, I never took a single vacation. I couldn't afford to go on vacation. Then, little by little, we started to take a long weekend to Galveston or week in a cabin close to the DFW Metroplex (home). When things started to change, though, they changed pretty dramatically. In the past two years, my family has taken vacations to Five-Star resorts in Florida, The Bahamas, Dublin, Scotland, Paris, and Rome. Every time that I do, I make at least a couple of videos.

The top two of these examples were shot by my eight-year-old daughter with my snapshot camera: http://www.leadersinstitute.com/public-speaking/videos.html

Your videos don't have to be fancy, but it is worth the investment to hire a professional videographer to record and edit your videos. Videographers are in an interesting business, because they charge a huge fee to do events, but when they are not doing big "events" they are often idle (which is why they have to charge so much for their event time).

A fun experiment is to call one and ask them to film a three hour wedding and reception on a Saturday night. You'll get quoted thousands and thousands of dollars. Then call back later and ask them how much it would cost you to hire them for three hours on a Tuesday morning. Their fee will likely be very small in comparison. The reason why is that folks who specialize in weddings are pretty idle throughout the weekdays, so if they can pick up some extra work, they jump at the opportunity.

Just like with any industry, though, you get what you pay for, so if the fee is too cheap, the product will probably be cheap as well.

Regardless of how you create or distribute your videos, make sure and start the process. You'll get lots of activity on your websites and help people in the process.

Chapter 8:
Five Big Mistakes that will Ensure that Someone who Contacts You will Buy from Someone Else

So you've worked really hard to get tons of new people looking at your website and all of those great leads start flowing in. Now the most important part takes place. You have to turn those leads into revenue.

Unfortunately, this is the part at which most entrepreneurs fail miserably. Most small business owners have an expertise in their own industry, but they often don't have a lot of first-hand sales experience – especially when they are first starting out.

Below are some of the most common mistakes that entrepreneurs make in the follow up process. Avoid them, and you close a higher percentage of your leads that 80% of your competitors.

Mistake #1: Thinking that All of Your Leads are Ready to Buy Right Now

Remember that just because people who search you out have a challenge or a problem, doesn't mean that they will be ready to buy right now. However, if you keep in touch with them, avoid pressuring them to buy, and continue to educate them, they will often come to you when they are ready to buy.

For instance, in my own company, we offer corporate team building events. Most of these events take place at conventions or annual meetings. The event planners start to gather information sometimes six to 12 months before the event. In the early stages, though, the event planners just want to know what is out there – what are their options.

What our sales team will do with this type of prospect is help educate them on the different options that they have available and then give them ammunition to help them persuade the other people on their committee. Our team will ask a lot of questions and then customize the materials that they send to the prospect to try to ensure that the materials are helpful for them. If they find out that the committee will be meeting in a month, the will call the prospect a couple of days before the meeting and make sure that the person has the correct information and then coach the person on how to persuade coworkers.

It is a process, and in every step of the process, the salesperson is building the relationship. Even if the salesperson doesn't close the deal this time, guess what? The group will be doing another event next year, so the salesperson can now start the process again and help them with the next event.

Our sales team does a great job consulting with potential clients versus sinking the sales fangs in and not letting go.

Granted, though, if you are getting thousands of leads every month, it will be impossible to follow up in detail with every single lead forever. You will also need some type of automated follow up system so that no one falls through the cracks.

An email follow up system can save you a lot of time.

"An email follow up system can save you a lot of time."

There are a ton of email follow up systems out there. Constant Contact is the one that you see and hear the most about, and it is a great email follow up system. However, an email follow up system can save you a lot of time if it is integrated with your CRM (Customer Relationship Management software – A database that keeps track of your clients and leads) and your website. There are specific follow up systems that do all of these things and are designed specifically for small businesses as well.

The one that I use is called InfusionSoft. It's the third CRM system that we have used, and it is, by far, the easiest and most useful that I've come in contact with. You basically set up a form through the InfusionSoft interface and just paste a few lines of code onto your website. Once you do, any time someone comes onto your website and request information or enters their email address, all of their information gets inserted into your CRM and an automatic email follow up system will start that can continue for years if you want it to.

You can find information about InfusionSoft at http://www.tli-infusionsoft.com.

Regardless of what follow up system that you use, you have to have one.

Mistake #2: Giving Up on Leads

Most professional salespeople give up on prospects before they turn into business. Most entrepreneurs have even less of a closing ratio, but if you change the way that you follow up with your potential clients, you can turn things around very quickly.

When an initial lead comes in, for instance, someone comes onto a website and requests information via a form on the website, most small business people will do one of these things.

Most entrepreneurs will likely email the prospect with tons of sales literature and follow up via email a dozen times or so, and then quit trying with a "that's not a real prospect after all" mentality.

Others might make a phone call and leave a voicemail and just wait for the person to call back.

Others will call and leave a voicemail and wait. Then call back and leave another voicemail. Then call back and leave another voicemail. And when the client doesn't call back, they quit trying with a "that's not a real prospect after all" mentality.

A very few will send out an expensive sales kit to the client via FedEx and wait a week or two to call them again hoping that the sales kit closes the deal.

By the way, any of those techniques will work every once in a while, but none of them will close a high percentage of deals for you.

A better process is to create different tiers of potential leads.

The first tier might be what I call email address leads. These are people who got free information from you and gave you their email address in return. If all you have is their email address, then you only have one way to follow up with them. So create an email follow up system in your CRM that combines education (information that they need) with offers to buy stuff from you. You might want to start with something small and build on it. If you are using a CRM system with an automatic email follow up, your follow up is turn-key.

The second tier might be website form leads. This is where someone comes onto your website and fills out a form requesting information or a call back from you. These are much higher quality leads, so they deserve a phone call. They are more likely to close more quickly, so be persistent in getting them on the phone. Don't just leave a voicemail and wait. Based on your conversation with them, you can determine whether you want to create more follow up calls with the person or just divert them over to your email follow up system.

Your highest tier might be call-in leads. Typically, when people call you, they want immediate results, so they will close much more quickly. Spend more time with these folks and follow up with them one-on-one for a longer period of time. Don't quit on these leads.

Whatever system you decide to use, DON'T QUIT! They requested information from you for a reason. You can help them.

Mistake #3: Giving a Sales Pitch

I mentioned this early in the book, but it is important to repeat. Don't deliver prospects a standardized sales pitch. Instead, find out

why they requested information from you. Once they tell you their problem, oddly enough, they will assume that you can solve the problem.

Here are a few phrases that will be gold for you.

- Do you mind if I ask you a few questions so that I have a better idea of what we should be talking about?
- So why are you interested in (fill in the blank with whatever product or service you sell)?
- Has something happened recently that has moved this up on your priority list?

Those should help you get started on the right foot with your new prospect. The more that they talk, the more they will want to buy from you. Fight the urge to jump in when you see an opportunity to sell to them.

Example:

Business Owner: "Do you mind if I ask you a few questions so that I have a better idea of what we should be talking about?"

Prospect: "I guess so..."

Business Owner: "So why are you interested in getting some advertising specialties made for your company?"

Prospect: "Well, the company that we bought pens from last time increased their charge and then messed up our website on the pens. We had to send them back, and we didn't have any for our big tradeshow."

Business Owner: "Well let me tell why that won't be a problem with our company..."

Arrggghh... That is a BIG mistake. Your prospect is now venting to you about how bad your competitor is. Don't cut her off. Encourage her to tell you more instead. Try something like...

Business Owner: "Gosh, that sounds terrible. What do you think that cost you?"

After she vents a little more, ask another question like, "Is there anything else about your current vendor that you'd like to improve?" etc. etc.

Continue asking questions until you feel like you have a few challenges that she has experienced that you think that you can fix for her.

Mistake #4: Making Price the Deciding Factor

When I was a teenager, my best friend's dad bought a Yugo car. The Yugo lasted on the market for, maybe a year or two, but went the way of the Edsel very quickly. This was a car that was made in Yugoslavia back when the Soviet Union was still in existence, and the main selling point for the cars was that they were being sold for about $5000, I believe.

The first (and last) time I rode in the Yugo, I was in the back seat, and Scott, my friend, pointed to the road and said, "Dad, WATER!" I'm freaking out, because I think we're about to drive into a lake, but it had just rained, and it was actually a dip with about four or five inches of water in it. My friends dad swerved, but ended up hitting the puddle anyway, and the car sputtered and died.

I was looking at the dad and then to Scott and then back to his dad, and I could see them both cursing under their breath. I finally said, "What just happened?"

Scott, gritting his teeth, said, "Any time this crappy car gets water up inside the engine block, for some reason it just dies. It is some kind of exposed electrical system, because unless we wait for the wires to dry out again, it won't start."

"So are we stuck here?"

Scott paused and said, "No we just have to jump start it."

I started laughing thinking he was joking, but he opened his door and directed me to get out. The three of us started pushing the car (which was incredibly easy by the way) and his dad jumped into the car and popped the clutch. The car sputtered but started.

The Yugo didn't last much longer than that. The point of the story is that most people don't buy the cheapest product or service. They don't trust the quality of the cheapest product.

However if the things that you tell your prospects are the same as what your competitors are saying, if your materials and literature are saying the same thing, if your website looks the same, then the only thing left to make a decision on is price. So now you have to determine a price that is not the cheapest, but competitive enough to not price you out of the market (Very hard to do).

The good news is that if you use your articles, videos, email campaigns, and initial phone calls to educate your prospect, you can almost name your own price, because you will have your prospect's trust, and they will know that you are worth the additional fee.

Mistake #5: Slow Follow Up

Yes, I know this was one of the original mistakes from the front of the book, but it's so important we're going to spend a whole chapter on it.

This one mistake is costing most companies who advertise on the web (which is just about every company out there) millions of dollars every year. Fix this one challenge, and you'll increase your income exponentially in the next 12 months.

Speed on the internet is the key to long term success!

Chapter 9:
Speed is the Key to Success

If you pull one secret to success from this book, make sure that it is this. When people look for information, products, or solutions on the internet, they want instant gratification. If they have to wait for you to send back an email or wait for a phone call from you, you've probably already lost them. If they have to wait for you to send them something in the postal mail, you never had a shot anyway.

The first time that I realized just how critical this was, I had been in business for a few years, and my company was a preferred vendor for a training website. Every day, people would visit this website, and because it was so comprehensive, it was very difficult to navigate. As a result, a lot of people would just fill out the form on the website requesting whatever type of training that they were looking for. As soon as someone filled out the form, it automatically got posted on the secure side, so if you were one of these preferred businesses, you could login at any time and see what had been posted.

To help us all out, though, the owner of the website would send out a summary at the end of the day, so every evening about 8:00 PM or so, we'd all get an email with a list of all of the leads that came in that day.

I responded to hundreds of these leads without any success whatsoever. Then, one evening, there was a lead for a public speaking class in Dallas. I thought, "Oh, I got this one." And I responded to it. The next morning, I called the person and introduced myself, and she was the most cold and distant prospect I think I have ever talked to. She just said, "We've already chosen someone else," and hung up. I was totally confused.

So I thought about what I should do to try and close some of these leads, and I figured that I really needed to know what everyone else was doing. So I went onto the site and created a posting of my own. It was about 10:30 AM, and I put into the posting that I would only accept email proposals.

By 11:00 AM, I had already received three proposals. The first was just a generic email with a HUGE attachment that took quite a while to download. It was about 20 MB of brochures in eight separate attachments that I never really went through. The second was just a simple email saying, "If you still need help, call me." (Okay it was a little more involved than that, but not much.) The third, though, was a beautiful, professional looking proposal. After glancing at it, I had pretty much decided that if I had really been buying a public speaking class, I would have hired that company.

By 3:00 PM, I had about 25 proposals.

By 6:30 PM, I had received almost 50 proposals.

By 8:00 PM, the time that I was typically receiving the summary email from the website, I had received over 72 proposals.

The next morning when I woke up, I had received 143 proposals. After the first 20 or so, I didn't look at any of them – not even out of curiosity.

When new proposals kept coming in the morning (less than 24 hours since I posted the listing,) they just ticked me off. I was thinking, "What a loser! You're number 150 on the list." But remember, that less than 24 hours prior, I was consistently number 73 or 74 on the list every single night.

I met with my team that day to share what I found out. We made a commitment to be the first to respond to every request. We only had six people working for the company, but we decided to assign one person every day just to wait for the phone to ring, one person just to wait for individual email leads to come in, and another just to wait for corporate contract requests to come in.

Our goal was to call any email inquiry back in less than five minutes. The most common comment that we started getting when we made those phone calls was, "Wow! I just hit send. You guys are really fast."

That year we went from a small half-million dollar company to almost one and a half million dollars. The next year we doubled sales again. The only thing that really changed was the speed at which we were following up with potential clients.

Typical Web Surfer

Typical web surfers will usually do something like this. They have a question and quickly do a Google search. They will scan the first page that pops up looking for a listing summary that most closely relates to what they are looking for. If they find one, they will click the link to see if an answer can be found.

Not finding the answer right away, they might fill out a web form requesting additional information.

Then they will go back to Google and look at the next listing. This one has an FAQ page, and they read a few of them and feel comfortable enough to fill out another form to get a second opinion.

Then they will go back to Google and look one more time. This time, the website has a blog with dozens of helpful articles and a few videos that look really nice. They now pick up the phone and end up getting a voicemail.

They might look at a few more listings, but most will not likely to fill out any more forms. No one wants to be bombarded with spam from a lot of websites, so they will probably be cautious about filling out more forms. They will probably only call additional listings from here on out and only if the website is very compelling.

So here is the big question...

Who is most likely to get the business?

If the owner of the third website had answered the phone instead of having the call go over to voicemail, then that person would have had a tremendous advantage over the other two companies. In fact, if the person replies to the voicemail right away, that owner still has an advantage.

In reality, the person who makes contact with the prospect first and builds rapport with the prospect is always in the driver's seat.

However, if you respond to the email the next day, the person will answer the phone saying, "Huh? Who are you again?" The person typically forgets entirely that he/she requested the information in the first place.

If the person gets a brochure in the mail a week after sending the email, well... you get the picture.

Speed is your friend in online sales. If you can't personally follow up on the requests, then hire someone. If you can't hire someone, then at least invest in a good email follow up system.

Don't make your good prospects wait for you.

Move quickly. Move nimbly. And make a ton of people happy and a ton of money in the process!

Chapter 10:
Final Thoughts

This information in this book can be very valuable once it is applied in the "real world." However, one of the biggest challenges that you are likely to find is that if you try one of these techniques, and it doesn't work exactly the way you are expecting, it's easy to get discouraged and look for another way to get to your result.

By the way, that process is what makes us an entrepreneur. We're always looking to improve on the status quo. One of the best ways that I've ever found to apply new processes or skills is with a coach. One thing that every professional athlete has in common is that every single one of them has a good coach. Most successful business people have a coach or mentor as well. There is no reason to make the same mistakes that other people who have been in your position have made.

Once Rick came on board with me as my first real employee, the growth of my company started to accelerate. The more that I surrounded myself with other experts, the faster the company grew.

What I figured out in hind-sight, though, was that the experts were always around me, but I thought of all of them as competitors. You have experts around you as well. Each of these experts have resources that you probably need, and you have resources that they need. When you begin to create mastermind groups with these other experts, you can learn their best practices and they can learn yours.

Your growth rate will increase dramatically.

One of the main reasons why people attend *the Small Business Lead Generation in a Digital Age* seminar for which this book was written, is that it gives them the platform to network with like-minded people who are looking to accomplish similar things with their business. They also get access to the coaching groups and one-on-one time with the instructors.

I'd encourage you to attend the next seminar in your area, because in the seminar, we take the theoretical information and make it very practical and turn-key for you.

For details, visit the Entrepreneur Boot Camp website at http://www.leadgenerationbootcamp.com.

By the way, this book and seminar is just **Part One** of the **Five Part Leader's Institute® Entrepreneur Boot Camp** series. Below are the additional topics:

Part #2: Generating an Irresistible Offer in Social Media

Generating an Irresistible Offer in Social Media (Advertising Strategies in a Digital Age) is a fantastic workshop that offers a number of time-tested advertising strategies that will help you maximize your revenue from pay-per-click advertising, your website pages, Facebook, Twitter, and YouTube accounts. If you've ever lost money advertising on the internet or sending out direct mail pieces that flopped, then this

small business seminar will be a blessing for you. We'll show you big mistakes that entrepreneurs often make when they advertise and how to avoid them. We'll also show you how to create advertising that will generate a high return on your investment!

Part #3: Eliminating Public Speaking Fear to Generate New Customers/Clients

No doubt about it. The person who stands up in front of a group of people and speaks with poise and self-confidence is always seen as being the leader and the expert in the industry. The problem is that 95% of the population has some kind of public speaking fear so, odds are, when you stand up to speak, you're going to feel the butterflies in the stomach and sweaty palms. This workshop is based on the Fearless Presentations® public speaking seminar that has helped tens-of-thousands of people eliminate public speaking fear. This workshop is specifically designed to help entrepreneurs and small business owners use public speaking opportunities to generate rapport with an audience so that a business relationship between the speaker and the audience can develop.

Part #4: Creating Key Small Business Alliances to Feed Leads and Referrals

One of the biggest mistakes that small business owners make is that we try to be the Lone Ranger and "go it alone," because we are often strong, and self-confident individuals. However, if you want to increase your growth exponentially, create non-competitive business alliances with other small businesses that will benefit from your services and who you can also benefit from their services. For instance, realtors can go out and place flyer after flyer on doors, or they can partner with a mortgage broker, an insurance agent, a remodeler, and more to create a team of entrepreneurs who can help each other grow. These alliances are critical to fast growth, and if you invite your potential alliance partners to the seminar as well, your team will be on the fast track to additional revenue streams.

Part #5: Small Business Leadership Strategies – Become the Industry Expert

As your business grows and you start hiring employees, it's important to create a team culture within your organization and surround yourself with confident leaders throughout your small business. Since most entrepreneurs don't have an unlimited training budget or a fully staffed HR team, we often have to create this culture on our own. This workshop will help you hire the right people for the right job, coach and motivate your team, and grow your employees into the next generation of leaders for your company. Ever wonder why the people that you hire take their time to complete simple and easy tasks? Ever wonder why your team isn't as ambitious as you are? It might be your company structure or it might be that you are hiring the wrong people. This workshop will show you how to fix these and other leadership problems.

For details about any of these seminars or other books like this, visit the Entrepreneur Boot Camp website at http://www.leadersinstitutebootcamp.com.

Success to you!

www.ingramcontent.com/pod-product-compliance
Lightning Source LLC
Chambersburg PA
CBHW060621200326
41521CB00007B/844